SUPER-PARENT SURVIVAL GUIDE

First published in Australia in 2004 by:
Pennon Publishing
Suite 1, 59 Fletcher St
Essendon 3040
www.pennon.com.au

The National Library of Australia
Cataloguing-in-Publication entry:

Hall, Dr Janet
The Parent Survival Guide

ISBN 1 877029 64 5

1. Child rearing. 2. Parent and child. I. Title.

649.1

Designed by Allan Cornwell
Printed in Australia by McPhersons Printing Group

Enquires to be made to:
Dr Janet Hall
Accelerated Success Centre
69 Erin St, Richmond, Vic 3121
Phone: 61 3 9429 1677
www.drjanethall.com.au
email: info@drjanethall.com.au

SUPER-PARENT SURVIVAL GUIDE

DR JANET HALL

PENNON
PUBLISHING
2004

CONTENTS

Meet the Author

Dr Janet Hall is a mother, clinical psychologist, speaker, hypnotherapist, and best-selling author.

Her books include:

How You Can Be Boss of the Bladder, Easy Toilet Training,
Fear-free Children, Fight-free Families,
Sex-Wise: What Every Parent and Teenager Needs To Learn About Sex and,
Sex-Life Solutions: Easy Ways to Solve Everyday Sex Problems.

Janet has a happy knack of giving common-sense ideas and time-saving strategies for busy caring parents and clever kids!

Meet the Illustrator

Neil Matterson is the editorial cartoonist for the second largest newspaper in circulation in Australia, the Brisbane *Sunday Mail.*

ATTENTION PARENTS AND HELPING PROFESSIONALS

There are many excellent textbook overviews of parenting and children's problems but these are usually very technical. This new book offers a 'cook-book' approach which empowers parents by having solutions readily available at times of crisis.

ATTENTION FRIENDS AND FAMILY

The *Super-Parent Survival Guide* could save someone's sanity. Be a life-saver and give a copy to someone that you care about today! All new mums and dads especially deserve a *Super-Parent Survival Guide*!

SURVIVAL GUIDES ARE LIFE SAVERS

If you don't have exactly all the right equipment, you can still create your own uniquely safe environment using *flexibility*!

Don't say what won't work!

It's not necessary to *adopt* every strategy.

Feel free to … *adapt– create – celebrate.*

HOW TO USE THIS BOOK

Why the *survival guide* approach to parent/child problems?

Because the Super-Parent is a myth!

Parents are busy people – especially when their children are very young.

This is the time when you most need to think carefully about your reactions to the challenges of child-raising. But you are usually under pressure having to make instant decisions in chaotic conditions.

FOR BUSY PARENTS: Busy parents don't have time to read a text book or consult an expert when there is a crisis.

The *Super-Parent Survival Guide* has instant strategies for handling child problems which are a quick referral source for challenged parents. Keep it on your kitchen bench or in your car or anywhere handy.

It can be a valuable resource for ideas and also for regaining your sense of humour and equilibrium!

And consulting it can be an opportunity to calm down and *not* do something you might regret!

A key aspect of this book is that parents are made accountable for their own behaviour first. Children learn from watching you, so you have to model what you want them to learn.

CONGRATULATIONS!

And thank you for using this guide.

You deserve acknowledgment for being a concerned parent:

– whose time is valuable

– who is already doing a great job

– who cares about your kids

– who values positive, easy, economical parenting skills

– who wants your kids to be appropriately independent

The *Super-Parent Survival Guide* is in two sections:

PART ONE — Survival Guide Essential Knowledge

- The truth about parenting
- The 4 'C' keys to positive parenting
- Use loving firmness
- The 3 'D' secret strategies for a counter attack.

In Part One it is strongly recommended that you pay particular attention to:

- **The 4 'C' Keys – Copying, Cues, Consequences and Compassion, plus:**
- **The 3 'D' secret strategies – Detach, Distract and Defy**

These strategies are the basis for handling the A-Z problems in section two so you need a clear understanding of each.

PART TWO — A-Z Strategies For Handling Child Problems

Part Two contains the A-Z of problems that allow you *instant* referral at times of crisis!

PART ONE
ESSENTIAL KNOWLEDGE

THE TRUTH ABOUT PARENTING

1. Parenting is the toughest job we ever have to do! *and yet*…we get no direct training in it.

2. Parenting is learned from *copying*: parents need to model the best behaviour for children to copy.

3. Parents do the best they can with the information they have available at the time.

4. Everybody else is an expert on parenting and can always be relied on to tell you what you are doing wrong.

5. Trust your own judgment.

6. Be flexible – Be adaptable – Do whatever works for you!

7. Remember: *For things to change, first I must change.*

Parents also need to learn that sometimes children can be contrary and no matter how logical a behavioural option might seem to the parent . . . the child will take the other. For example, a child who has been doing well at a hobby, say karate, might suddenly decide that he does not want to pursue that hobby any more.

THE 4 'C' KEYS TO POSITIVE PARENTING

There are four key influences on our behaviour.

1. Copying — parents need to model the best behaviour for children to copy.

Parenting is usually modelled from what our parents did to us or what we pick up from TV, magazines and books.

2. Cues — signals, reminders, arrangements, rules and routines. We learn by doing what we are told and getting into good habits which are consciously and unconsciously repeated and triggered off by reminders, signals, arrangements, routines and agreements.

We create our own rules and rituals for our families. We develop new ones and sometimes we borrow from the memories of our own growing up with our parents.

3. Consequences — rewards and punishment.

A behaviour that is rewarded will increase.

A behaviour that is punished will decrease.

The type of consequences that our parents applied – rewards or punishments – may have been inconsistently imposed, depending very much on their mood at the time.

4. Compassion — being understood and listened to = caring communication.

Parenting is the hardest job we ever have to do

And the one job that we get no training in!

If we get no training in parenting, how is it that we know how to parent? We learn from our own parents!

Whenever I ask a group of parents how many people promised themselves (at least once) when they were little kids, that 'I'll never do what my parents did to me!', they nearly all raise their hands! Now they find themselves, when they have kids, *doing exactly what their parents did* to them, even though they swore they never would!

Parenting can be made much easier for us if we learn to apply, by choice, the aspects of parenting our parents may have applied haphazardly. Used wisely, the major principles of learning offer the path to a calm and happy family.

Parents and family history

It may be time for you to stop and analyse your family situation. Have you copied your parenting style from your own parents? Are you reacting to your children the way your parents reacted to you when you wanted to have independence?

It's time to take responsibility. You may still choose to be exactly the kind of parent that you are now. And that's OK. Just be sure that you are being that parent through choice . . . and not through an unconscious drive to continue the same pattern or react in the opposite way, just to prove a point.

1. COPYING

Parents need to model the best behaviour for children to copy.

You are your child's most significant model.

You must be the person you want your child to be.

- Choose your friends wisely
- Keep your space clean
- Keep fit and healthy
- Tell the truth
- Keep your life organised
- Keep your sense of humour
- Be resilient– bounce back with a positive attitude after adversity
- Control your bad moods – don't over-react.

Children, like adults, learn from what they see other people do. We don't have to actually have experiences ourselves. Modelling comes from things that we read, things that we watch on television and movies and things that we see others do and hear others say.

Children who observe adults abusing themselves – by staying up late or drinking alcohol, watching too much television, leading sedentary lives, no exercise, over-eating, smoking, and taking drugs – are likely to copy these behaviours.

Parenting Models to Avoid

Suzie, aged 5, had a phobia about spiders. She would run screaming from any tiny creature with spidery features. Suzie's mother was also scared of spiders and would pick her up and run hysterically from the house, refusing to go back inside until the spider had been removed.

Marie, aged 11, was always complaining about a sore tummy and headaches, and was scared to try anything new. Marie's mother was scared of every single thing, it seemed, but most of all that something bad would happen to Marie. The mother had been deserted by her husband when Marie was only 6 months old. Mother had then poured all her love and attention onto Marie. At the age of 11 Marie had never slept overnight at a friend's house. Her mother picked her up every day straight after school. The mother needed psychological treatment to enable her to cope day by day with her fears that something bad would happen to Marie whilst she was at a camp!

2. CUES

The key strategy to prevent child behaviour problems is to have the 4 R's!

Rules
Regulations
Routines
Rituals

Just watch children meet – they don't even need to know each other's names, but they immediately select roles and rules. For example, if they are playing a game about a family, they say 'You're the mother, I'm the father *and these are the rules*!'

The importance of rules

- We give orders, set rules and help when we know for sure our children cannot handle a problem by themselves.
- We give orders, rules and help when we feel life and limb are in definite danger.

Unclear rules or routines

Children often fight over 'whose turn is it?' Fighting can reach fever pitch in no time at all when emotions are involved, especially when kids think something is unfair. Picture the following scenario:

'Whose turn is it to feed the dog?' asks Mum. The two children both look at each other and scream as loudly as possible, 'Not mine? Must be his/hers'.

Mum can't remember whose turn it is and so says to the eldest one, 'It must be your turn'.

Eldest one says, 'Why do you always pick on me Mum, you always pick on me – you never pick on him. Why does he get his own way? What about last week when you drove him to school and you wouldn't let my friend come over to play? You're a rat Mum!'

Mum's blood starts to boil. 'Don't speak to me in that tone of voice', she says.

Children may dispute parents' rules but they do respect the system of rules. Rules are the roadmaps to communication because they establish agreements. Children need to grasp the fundamental importance of keeping agreements if they are to become responsible adults.

There are a few very important guidelines for creating rules

- Keep the rules short and simple – what is wanted and when it should be done by.
- Phrase the rules in a positive tone – state what you want them to do not what you don't want them to do.
- Post the rules early to avoid disputes. The best and most convenient place to post the rules is the greatest art gallery in the world – the family refrigerator!
- Create the rules together with the children, don't dictate!

Rules can help prevent fights if they show:

- Whose turn it is to feed the cat, sit in the front seat, open the drink bottle, turn on TV…
- What is expected before school, before bedtime.
- How to pack up.
- If you are in doubt as to whether a rule is necessary, just look for the moments of hottest dispute – that's when rules can prevent pain!

Explaining new rules

Because rules do apply differently, according to the chronological age and maturity of your children, it is important that parents clearly communicate rule changes. The transition from being 'mummy's little helper' to being a person with regular domestic chores may not be easily digestible. The 'righteous little boy/girl' syndrome occurs (this is a set of symptoms characterised by extreme anger when asked to do something, claims of 'it's not fair', 'it's not my turn', 'why should I do it' and 'I didn't ask to be born').

How well does it have to be done?

Once you have your rules and requirements you need to make them very specific so there can never be a dispute about the expected standards. If you don't make your standards clear you are likely to get 'righteous little child' syndrome. Things to watch out for include:

Toddlers – 'I cleaned up my room' means . . . doona pulled up over the top of a pile of one dirty sock, one used handkerchief, one tennis racquet, one stick with nails in it and one half of an apple.

Teens – 'I cleaned up my room' means . . . the same amount of stuff that a toddler might leave, except this time it is all under the bed.

A chore and pocket money system

Setting up a checklist which specifies what chores need to be done, by when and what the reward will be, is highly recommended. This kind of system prevents us from having to constantly give instructions. As any parent every day will find, unless there is a system with checklists, children will always find excuses.

3. CONSEQUENCES

Parenting power comes from careful use of consequences.

Most parents think that they do a good job of rewarding children most of the time. Parents are usually reluctant to punish their children, reserving punishment for dangerous or decidedly naughty behaviours, *but* . . . most parents do not know the truth about rewards and punishments.

All behaviour has a payoff!

Rewards – increase behaviour

Punishers – decrease behaviour

These scientifically proven principles of behaviour stand out as the two most important things that I learned from studying psychology.

If you think you are punishing your children for stealing from your purse by smacking them, and they are still stealing . . . then smacking is not a punisher and you should stop it straight away.

If you think that rewarding your child with praise will ensure that homework is done but the homework is not done . . . it is time to find a more effective reward.

The reward rule

People keep doing things that make them feel better

The punishment rule

People stop doing the things that don't make them feel better or that make them feel worse

When rewarding children, remember: a reward is only a reward if it increases a behaviour. Ask what the child would: work for, co-operate with, be willing to do, or suffer with, in order to have what they want. Then, parents can identify immediately if a reward really is a reward by watching to see if the behaviour they think that they were rewarding increases.

Assume nothing

For example, if you give a child a jellybean every time they eat up their dinner and a jellybean is a reward for your child – you would expect that finishing of meals would increase (without any fights or upsets). Just like you worked for a pay cheque the child works to get their jellybean. Watch and see if it works!

Warning: Not all children are rewarded by a jellybean. Some children don't like sweets! Just because one child loves black jellybeans, don't expect that the next child will love black jellybeans. They might have a preference for sultanas – yes, many children now prefer healthy natural foods, rather than confectionery.

Congratulations to all those parents whose conscientious intention to educate their children to make healthy choices in food has paid off.

Parent attention is usually a reward

Some parents are actually rewarding when they think they are punishing. If you think that you are punishing a child by applying something which you think they don't like, please check to see if it is a punishment by watching to see if that behaviour decreases.

For example, many people believe that smacking their children works. If you find that you are smacking your children more and more because they speak cheekily or rudely to you but their bad language continues unabated then your smacking behaviour may actually be a reward!

Remember, smacking can be a reward because it gives a child attention and attention is rewarding.

What helps rewards work?

Rewards work best when they are applied consistently and closely follow (in time) the behaviour that you want to increase.

The druther rule – Use things that children like to do as a reward for things they don't like to do. For example, some people might druther be outside relaxing on a hot day than inside working on their accounts. Is there anything you would druther be doing right now than reading this book?

A 'druther' works like this: An eight and a half year old who'd druther watch TV . . . needs to be reminded that he is not able to watch TV unless his room is clean. The TV (liked) is the reward for the clean room (disliked).

Remember: At adolescence, reward values change

At the onset of adolescence, everything about rewards changes.

Teenagers scoff at what they perceive to be patronising parent praise. Usually the only rewards a parent can offer a teenager are to do with money and free time – free time to spend with their friends of course!

Visual tracking rewards

Children may all vary in their choice of what they find rewarding, but most seem to enjoy visual tracking rewards. For instance, by colouring in or putting a sticker on a spot on the dinosaur for each day they have a dry bed, the children who are in our clinic's How You Can Be Boss of the Bladder program are motivated to have even more dry nights.

Parents can use this strategy to encourage children to have fight-free and yell-free days. Perhaps parents could challenge themselves to join in and have their own spot chart for a nag-free day!

The progressive reward of completing a spot results in a very colourful picture which is an incentive for the child and a reward in itself.

Punishment

Physical punishment

Includes anything which physically hurts: smacking, scratching, biting, hitting with an object, strapping, shaking.

Withdrawal of a positive – includes: taking away TV privileges, going to bed early, being grounded, not being able to see your friends or not having sweets, time out.

Verbal punishment – includes:

Criticism: 'Why couldn't you do that properly, are you stupid?'

Labelling: 'Yes you are a stupid idiot'

Nagging: 'Will you do it?' 'I said will you do it?' 'I said *will you do it?'*

Ridicule: 'You'll never be able to do that'

Note: Tone of voice can also be punishing – screaming, groaning, threatening, sarcasm, lecturing and swearing.

A punisher is only a punisher if it works.

Parents who keep yelling, nagging, and smacking often believe that the punishment is working because they momentarily get the child to stop the behaviour. If parents were to watch for a while though, they may observe that over a period of time the misbehaviour is not decreasing. The punishment is only temporarily effective.

Is punishment a good model?

There is a classic cartoon where the father is hitting the young boy and screaming out 'I'll teach you to hit your brother'. Every time a parent punishes they are modelling punishment and it's likely that their children will learn from this model. Do you want your children to hit their kids?

Punishment can lead to fear, resentment and escape. No doubt you can still remember a time when an adult who was much more powerful than you punished you for something you didn't do. It's probable that you were seething with indignation, frustration, and helplessness.

A young child will eventually learn to fear an adult who punishes them frequently. As the fear builds up, internal resentment also builds up and the child may become extremely rebellious or alternatively retreat into their own world.

Applying punishment – ideal conditions

Psychologists have studied the phenomenon of punishment extensively and have concluded that punishment only works when five conditions are met. It must be done:

1. Immediately
2. Consistently
3. By a cool and calm administrator
4. With absolutely no way out for the victim
5. At very intense and painful levels

These conditions may exist in an experimental laboratory but how on earth can they be controlled in a family situation? In real life it's actually very hard for a parent to be able to meet the five basic conditions for making punishment work.

It's almost impossible to consistently and immediately administer punishment and kids know many ways out! Kids are masters at not being caught. And even if they are caught they usually escape the consequences. Just think: How fast can you run? How much faster than you can your child run? How embarrassed would you feel if you were seen in public chasing a naughty child through the streets?

How cool and calm can a tired and exhausted parent remain? Some naughty behaviour may provoke even the coolest parent.

Would you be able to remain cool and calm if your child had spilt paint all over the carpet, especially if you had warned the child about not even going near the paint tin and had put the paint tin very carefully – you thought – out of the child's reach and way up on a shelf in the garage?

In summary, the requirements for effective punishment are very demanding. It would be fair to say that applying punishment puts both parent and child at risk – the risk of hurting and being hurt. And even after all that disharmony, you may still not achieve the result that you wanted.

For all these reasons, rewards are always more attractive than punishment. If you do use punishment – be realistic, be aware, and beware.

If you must administer punishment

Give a warning in advance. Describe the situation positively: 'When you tidy your room you may then watch TV' instead of 'if you're not going to tidy your room then I'm not going to let you watch TV.' Make sure the punishment is appropriate for the behaviour and the person on the receiving end. Make sure punishment is given as close as possible in time to the behaviour. Follow through after your warning. Insist on action from the child, not promises of 'I won't do it again'. Don't get into an argument with the child.

When is punishment necessary?

There are some times when punishment is probably necessary and appropriate. These are:

When the behaviour is life-threatening and has to stop.

When there is a total 'no win' situation for both parties and new behaviour has to start somehow.

Life threatening behaviour

All parents have known the spine chilling fear of watching a small child run onto the road. You get a similar feeling when you see a child with a long pointy object probing a power point. At such times fear takes over and the parent usually smacks the child and calls out sharply.

The sharp smack and calling out actually meet most of the requirements for effective punishment. That is, the punishment is immediate, there is no way out and it gives the child an intense shock and probably pain. The problem with this punishment is that the parent is certainly not cool and calm. Try to stay cool!

Time out

The time-out technique is sometimes misunderstood. It really means time out from positive reinforcement, that is, not being allowed to have anything positive or rewarding happen to or around you. Implementing it can be fraught with problems as soon as the child is old enough to refuse to be put anywhere.

Organise a time-out space

Find a spot in the house which doesn't contain fun things for the child to do.

The child must be small enough or non-violent enough to go to the time-out space without a physical fight.

The child should be compliant enough to stay until given permission to leave. Be careful about locking your child in the room. This is advisable only under professional supervision.

If the child is likely to have a tantrum in the room, you must be able to prevent breakage.

Anything dangerous or poisonous must be well out of the way of the child.

Steps to follow to make time-out work:

1. The instant your child begins a tantrum, say, 'time out' and take your child to that time-out spot.
2. Make no other comment.
3. Do take the child to time-out every time the behaviour occurs. After a few minutes, (a good rule of thumb is number of minutes per age, i.e. two minutes for two-year olds, five minutes for five-year olds), let the child come out. If the child is still having a tantrum extend the time-out period until the child stops.
4. If the tantrum started when you asked the child to do something, repeat the request so that the child does what is asked.
5. Keep repeating the procedure as necessary.

With older children

If your child is too old to go where you send him or her, you may have to be the one who leaves the room. Follow the same procedure only every time your child has a tantrum, you leave the area. If your child makes any comment as you leave, just simply say, 'I don't have to listen to that'.

Combine rewards and punishment

Reward the good behaviour and ignore the bad behaviour

This is easier said than done. When you choose to ignore, initially, the behaviour may get worse! To many parents, the 'worse' lasts much longer than patience can bear.

Experts assure us that if you wait things will get better – but how can you wait for children to tidy their rooms when your mother-in-law is arriving on the doorstep in five minutes time? The answer to this dilemma is to combine rules, routines and removal of rewards or privileges.

Rules: your room must be clean in the morning before you go to school. A checklist posted on the wall shows exactly what 'clean' means.

Routines: The Silent Robot Box collects anything messy still left after the children leave for school.

Removal of rewards/privileges: No TV that night.

No treats: This can be different for every home. In our family it means no sweets, biscuits, soft drinks, TV, or friends over to play.

Early bedtime: As well as 'No Treats', children must stay in their bedroom after dinner.

Make-up: Everyone appreciates a chance to 'make-up' after a mistake. 'Making-up' is not always easy (e.g. supervising a child to clean up a spilt messy drink) but we learn the positive behaviour –*what to do* – in making-up. So, teach children *what to do*, not *what not to do*. If they can make-up, they feel better than being punished.

Strategy Summary for Parents

Cues to use

Record forms and checklists

Labelling things and areas

Timing – the timer is your best friend e.g. if a child is on the phone, the timer rings after 10 minutes.

Consequences to use

Negative Consequences

Ignore

Remove the object – put the special puzzle away

Remove bodies – children go to time out

Parents withdraw to their sanctuary (the toilet is your last resort)

Remove privileges, no TV, early bedtime

Positive Consequences

Reward positive behaviour

Praise

Lucky dip

Visual motivator (sticker sheets)

Special activities – mummy time, can play with precious toy (parents keep this toy e.g. jigsaw puzzle hidden and brought out on special occasions)

Consequences to avoid

Name calling, criticising, labelling

Nagging

Yelling and screaming

Hitting and threatening

Bribes – don't give something before the behaviour you want happens e.g. don't say 'Here's a lolly now stop screaming'. Do say, 'If you can play happily for 5 minutes you can have a lolly'.

Remember

Always follow through and be consistent. Remember, do as you say! Never make a threat to deliver a consequence if you cannot keep that threat. For example if you say, 'if you don't do these sums now, I'll never help you with your homework again . . .' and then you do help . . . If you say, 'if you leave home this time, you are never welcome back' . . . and then you keep their room impeccable and make their favourite food so that they will visit – you will lose all credibility, love and respect and you will perpetuate the child's bad behaviour. They will know they can wrap you around the proverbial little finger. They will continue to cause drama and get their own way.

Teach children 'what to do', not 'what not to do'!

Teach your children to share and co-operate and reward them for it!

Use firm consequences early. Avoid the upsets caused by no discipline, no co-operation and harassed parents.

Remember: *Short-term pain = long term gain*

'Firm parenting' now, will result in 'responsible children' later.

Short-term gain e g: giving in to your children's demands, will lead to long-term pain e g: your children will not co-operate and will keep demanding.

The 3 'D' secret strategies for a 'kids counter-attack'

Skilful parents use YGOLOHCYSP.

What's that? REVERSE PSYCHOLOGY!

Kids are master of 3 behaviours: Detach, Distract and Defy.

If kids can do them, parents can do them too!

1. Detachment

Kids can completely and totally *ignore* you – so copy from them!

e.g. Ignore them! Don't listen to them when they're demanding a biscuit!

How many times have you thought you have given your child a clear instruction, maybe to pack up the toy box and they completely seem oblivious to you, shut down or stone walling, oh boy are kids good at ignoring.

Well you used to be a kid too and you had that skill so you can get it back again. Don't give in! Put cotton wool in your ears if necessary but don't answer that whingeing for a biscuit, or that dob, that 'My little brother is teasing me.'

With true ignoring you are frozen, you have no eye contact, no verbal contact, you deep breathe, you are silent and your body signals are completely neutral. (It's certainly not the angry glare, the folded arms and the clenched fist that comes with saying No!)

Now I know it's not always completely possible to totally ignore a child because you have what's called 'a duty of care' to your child, especially if they're still only little.

So let's say it's the middle of the night and your toddlers come to your bed whingeing, whining and snivelling and wanting to get into your bed. The most courageous thing for an effective parent to do is to take the child back to his or her own bed, with as little pay-off as possible.

I repeat, with as little pay-off as possible, don't hug the child, don't croon to the child, simply carry the child back very neutrally and put the child back to bed.

2. Distraction

They can conveniently take your attention off what they didn't do and create a crisis diversion – so copy from them! e.g. Say 'Oh look at that beautiful bird in the sky'.

3. Defiance

Isn't it incredible what power those two little letters have, N O. It's one of the first words a toddler learns. Whenever a parent says, 'Put on your coat' ... It's 'No' – 'Get in the car'... 'No' – 'Sit on the potty' ... 'No.' – 'Give the toy to your sister'...'No'– 'Stop hitting the puppy' ... 'No.'

So what happened to us as parents, how come we can't say the word No and mean it, steadfastly, determinedly, with an iron will! They can say NO and totally and completely defy you – so copy from them! e.g. Say 'no' to them… and mean it!

4. COMPASSION

Children cannot think like adults.

It is hard for them to wait – if they want something they want it *now*!

Sometimes neither parents or children know why they behave abominably!

They might be *sick.*

They might be *tired.*

They might be *too young.*

They might be *feeling left out.*

They might be *frightened.*

So sometimes it's not appropriate for parents to be in control and implement consequences.

Your child may just need a cuddle and a love! So might you!

Use loving firmness

Balance between: 'Clearly allowing consequences to teach life's lessons' and 'Caring and understanding'.

For example: If the child forgets the school lunch – don't take it up to the school, but;

If the child has damaged his toy by leaving it out in the rain, give a cuddle and show you care.

A team approach

Children find it much tougher to manipulate, and more reassuring when they are really upset, to know that Mum and Dad have joined forces. Parents need to back each other up as much as possible, so that a routine is firmly kept. Sometimes it's difficult when one partner is working shifts or has an early start. But if you don't get a routine now, you may find battles may cause many hours of upset in the future. It's a case of *short-term pain* now for *long-term gain* later. Just make sure everyone agrees on how problems are handled, because you need to be consistent! The team must work together. Just check you have realistic expectations of your own situation and lighten up. Child misbehaviour can lead to parent/child battles, but you can win the war. Keep your team morale up by using your sense of humour.

Talking with children

Talking with children can be difficult because grown ups often forget that children are small and a lot of things can go over their heads. Do you remember how you felt as a child? What was important, what wasn't, what you understood and what you didn't, the people you liked, the people you didn't? Probably the people you liked were those who listened to what you had to say. Sometimes we don't listen to children – we talk down to them, we shout at them, we are too busy to talk to them or we give them all the answers (too soon).

- When your child really wants to talk to you, turn to face the child giving him/her all your attention. Don't keep on doing the dishes or try to carry on a conversation from the next room. Do turn the TV off.
- Listen without feeling the need to provide answers, lecture or criticise.
- Give some brief indication that you are interested and that you would like to hear more, e.g. 'uh hah, oh really, ooh'.
- In discussions with your children about what will happen if dangerous fighting occurs, you can teach them about 'early bedtime'. Children can 'make up' and avoid early bedtime if they can come up with an explanation and solution and way to make up.
- Make sure that you are hearing the child by briefly repeating back what you heard, but putting it in your own words.

A good listener is:

Attentive, interested, likeable and checks out the understanding of the information received to show that they really care, that they heard what the communicator wanted them to hear.

Sometimes parents listen to their children like their disinterested partner makes love; just lying there like a log, the body is present but there is no active participation. Kids want to see that their parents are animatedly interested and enthusiastic in what they have to say.

The most important thing parents can give their children is their time. The child needs to feel that the parent is thinking, 'You matter', 'Your feelings are important to me'.

For instance, if Johnny screams, 'Mum, he just called me an idiot and said I'm dumb'. If you tell Johnny, 'Just ignore it', he feels totally invalidated. It is important to say something like, 'He said a mean thing to you. I know that can hurt'. Remember, you have to identify with what happened and how the child feels.

How to Handle Kids' vs Parents' Problems

Whose problem is it?

A one-off fight in the school yard with other children is between the child and someone else and the parent should not be involved. It's a child problem. (An exception to this occurs when a child is being bullied – adults certainly should be involved here.)

However, if a child fights with his sibling in the living room while parents are watching (trying to watch?) TV and there's swearing and spitting going on, the parents have a problem and may step in. It's a parent problem and it's worth it.

The key distinction is whether there is an issue between parent and child which is directly affecting the parent – typically causing physical or emotional discomfort or breaking the parent's code of ethics/ standards. Then it's a parent problem.

How should parents handle children's problems?

1. Listening with understanding:

Say 'I know you need to get to the sports oval and it's raining. It's very disappointing that you will be late and wet by the time you get there'.

2. Letting consequences follow their natural course by not rescuing the child:

Say 'But because you slept in and you left your raincoat at school, you'll have to work out your own solution'.

3. Show love and concern. Say 'You deserve to play the game today because you trained hard and I'm very proud of your commitment'.

4. Ask 'What will you do *now*? What could you do to handle this situation?'

Anger from parents is not appropriate because it usually just makes everyone upset.

Examples of kids' problems and what parents can do

Homework – let the teacher/school handle it.

Clothes – the rule is you wash and iron your own, don't expect to go out with parents if you are wearing your old clothes.

Truancy – handle it with the school, community service office

Messy Room – use the Silent Robot technique.

Needs Transport – catch the bus, train, tram or negotiate.

The steps for handling a parent problem

1. Negotiate an agreement.

2. Insist with persistence and say:

   a) When you I feel/think …???

      What I want from you is …

      And what I'll do is …

b) I know you want … and I want …

3. Follow through consistently – No threats, you must do it.

4. Limited strike – So that kids experience the consequences, parents go on a mini-strike. This means the parent stops doing things for them – no money, no driving, no friends over…

Example: Handling a parent problem where kids talk back

Let's say the parents were upset because there was too much yelling and swearing between the kids and 'answering back' when parents made simple requests.

This issue causes upset to parents and directly involves them. Anger from parents may be appropriate. This doesn't mean you yell and swear back at them aggressively of course! It does mean, however, you can glare, flash your eyes and firmly insist:

Say 'No swearing or yelling – It's not *OK* in this house.'

1. *Negotiate an agreement*

Say 'If you wish to yell and swear, go to the local park!'

2. *Insist with persistence*

a) Say 'When you yell and swear, I get angry and sad and think you don't care about anybody else's feelings.What I want from you is that you speak about what you want without yelling and swearing and what I'll do is listen.

b) I know you want to let out your anger and I want peace in my house so you can let out your anger outside.

3. *Follow through consistently!*

4. *If necessary, go on a mini-strike*

Say: 'There's been too much yelling, swearing and answering back. I'm not cooking dinner until there's peace in this house.'

When should parents intervene?

Parents are not policemen but there are some situations when they, as responsible adults, must step in. These include:

- When a child's physical well being is at risk.
- When there is life damaging/threatening or degrading emotional violence.
- Where verbal abuse can be perceived as emotional abuse (constant put downs, name calling).
- Where a smaller child obviously has a disadvantage.
- When all the children ask for a family meeting, and in the early days to give feedback and make suggestions. e.g. 'How did it feel when Jodie called you an idiot? Tell him that hurt your feelings.'

PART TWO

AN A–Z OF COMMON PROBLEMS

AND THE STRATEGIES USED TO DEAL WITH THEM

ARGUMENTS

COPYING: Parents need to model the best behaviour for children to copy: Do you argue... loudly and often? Stop it. Learn to speak assertively and with intention. Remember this old saying: 'Never argue with a mug. An onlooker can't tell who's the mug'. Do you want your child to think you're a mug?

CUES: Have clear simple rules and routines e.g. Whose turn in front seat of car and whose to have the first bath. Anticipate likely crisis times: At meals, before school and before bed. If you can, keep your children separated!

CONSEQUENCES: Reward co-operation... frequently. If there is no co-operation use the 3 'D's.

1. Detach e.g. Parent leaves the room.
2. Distract e.g. Parent asks, 'Does anyone know how to open this packet of biscuits?'
3. Defy e.g. Parent says 'Stop arguing right now.'

COMPASSION: For yourself! Stay out of kids' arguments. Buy ear-muffs so you won't hear them. Encourage everyone to learn how to express their frustrations through 'Angry Actions'. These are explosive outbursts of energy e.g. Stamping foot, yelling out, running on the spot. To avoid frightening someone, before you do an angry action, you are obliged to signal it to your family, i.e. say 'Angry action coming up.'

Super-Parent Hot Tip

Arguing is not always a negative behaviour. We want our children to have their own opinions and feel that they are heard when they express them. It's an essential skill in having your own needs met and learning to be assertive. So never punish a child for objecting to an instruction.

If there is a priority for them to cooperate with your instruction however, say 'Please just do it now and we can talk it over tonight at dinner time'. Then make sure you keep your agreement and talk it over to show that the child's point of view has been heard.

Story

<u>The Problem</u>

Sally was embarrassed because her children were always arguing with her in front of other people. This was particularly bad when she went to pick them up from school in the afternoon and they would argue about about whose turn it was to sit in the front seat of the car. Sally could feel other parents looking at her to see what she would do. What made it worse was that Sally couldn't remember easily from day to day, whose turn it was next!

<u>The Solution</u>

Copying: Sally and her husband, Frank, agreed that they would not argue in front of the children. If one of them objected about the other's parenting, they would wait until they were alone to raise the issue and not contradict their partner in front of the children.

Cues: Sally needed a new rule where everyone could easily remember whose turn it was in the front seat. She asked the children what would work and nine year old Joel suggested that each child could sit in the front seat for a week at a time.

Consequences: If children were arguing, the parent would ignore it if it was brief and a solution was found. If it was intense, the parent would say 'Argue outside' and show the children to the door.

BULLYING & TEASING

COPYING: Parents need to model the best behaviour for children to copy: When you see someone being bullied, report it to an authority. Act promptly. Teach your child to be assertive but to get away from the bully as soon as possible. e.g. say 'Grow up' and walk away.

CUES: Bullies usually pounce in the streets and during breaks at school. So encourage your child to stay close to a friend and play near an authority figure at such times. Let your child learn a martial art like Karate, Tai Chi, Taikwando. Make sure they are responsible about using their skills and that they understand that discretion is the better part of valour!

CONSEQUENCES: Draw a picture of the bully – pin it up and throw spit balls* at it – cut it up into pieces and flush it down the toilet.

NB: *To make spit balls, simply tear up paper, roll the tiny bits into a ball and make them hard and tacky with your spit. Kids love it!

COMPASSION: Seek authority assistance – tell the teacher! Share your own experiences and tell your child stories of how heroes handled bullying.

Super-Parent Hot Tip

Teach your child to understand the right time to face up to conflict. Unfortunately many parents who avoid conflict are also teaching their children to avoid conflict.

By avoiding conflict we are creating a nation of 'nice' people who are unable to stand up for themselves. Fighting for what you believe in is important, but it should not be an aggressive win/lose painful fight. Instead you need to work through the appropriate channels by demonstrating, calmly and courageously, that you hold fast to what you believe in. If you do this you will have the best chance of getting what you want and making a positive difference.

It is this win/win kind of fighting that we want our children to learn. It all starts with letting children know that it's OK to express anger. Show them appropriate ways to do this; for example, punch the pillow. Let them know it's sometimes necessary to fight for what they want, but teach them how to negotiate and fight fair.

Teach your child how to react to conflict

We took our kids with us to Hawaii when they were just six and eight. They were minded during the day by a lovely lady and they were having a lot of fun but they were missing kids of their own age. I had what I thought at the time was a brilliant idea. Put them in an after school programme at a local Hawaiian school.

I expected to see beaming smiles when they came back but Pam was really upset and she said, 'Mum a kid called me a pig.' 'Oh that's terrible sweetie,' I replied, 'What did you do?' She said, 'Mummy, I told that boy what you taught me to say. I said, 'Thank you for sharing but I have another opinion!'

Well I tell you that's one of my best memories and I felt like a successful parent then. Pam had a ready reply that both put that mean kid 'back in his box' and affirmed her own self-esteem. She did have another opinion and she was proud of it.

So teach your child a coping saying. Feel free to use mine or make up one of your own.

Story

The Problem

Eight year old James complained of a sore tummy and a headache every day and did not want to go to school. His big sister told his parents that James was being bullied by a bigger boy in the street after school.

The Solution

Copying: James and his father enrolled in a martial arts class at the local community centre.

Cues: Dad arranged to drive James and Adam, a bigger boy who lived next door, to school in the morning. Adam agreed to walk home with James.

Consequences: The parents reported the bullying to the school principal, who investigated and found out the bully was a boy from another school. He alerted that school principal who then spoke to the bully's parents.

CRISIS AT PHONE TIME

COPYING: Parents need to model the best behaviour for children to copy: Do you interrupt others? Teach your children to respect other people's time by demonstrating that with your children. Tell them what you have to do and show them the time and give them a time limit that they must amuse themselves in whilst you are busy.

CUES: Invest in a portable phone so that you can go to a quiet place – if absolutely necessary, try the toilet!

Ideas for keeping toddlers busy

- give long-lasting food – (e.g. a bread crust with peanut butter):
- put TV on;
- put in play pen.

Keeping older children busy

Encourage free time:

- outside;
- in bedroom;
- special TV show or video which is only available when the parent wants time to concentrate on something.

CONSEQUENCES:

Detach – usually tough to do – hard to hear over the child's noise!

Distract – have a play phone – they ring their friends.

Defy – act – move the child – move yourself.

COMPASSION: For your call – arrange to call back later! Never make an issue of announcing that you want to make a call without interruption. You are just asking for it! Your request is actually a cue for the kids to do whatever they can to interrupt!

Super-Parent Hot Tip

The television is not a super-parent substitute. However it can be a useful baby-sitter if used for potentially crisis times such as when everyone is getting ready to go on an outing.

TV can help busy parents avoid drama. It's best to encourage children to be creative about activities and responsible for self-initiating them. Then, eventually, you don't have to be the indispensable parent who is always needed to organise an activity.

Try not to have the TV on in the morning. Growing children need to have their brains available then. If that's when the best shows are on, then videotape them and keep them for that terrible time before dinner.

Why don't you let your children watch a nature show that you have especially video taped for them. If you don't have a video, plan for parent time around a show that you do want your children to watch.

WARNING

TV babysitting willy-nilly is not recommended. Planned selected viewing however, can be a very useful babysitter. The pre-requisite is planning. Parents are encouraged to make sure they take responsibility to get the quiet time that they deserve.

DEMANDING & NAGGING

COPYING: Parents need to model the best behaviour for children to copy. Do you ask nicely, clearly and with respect? Demonstrate reliability: keep your agreements. Show respect for authority figures (the law, teachers) and don't undermine them in front of your children.

CUES: Make a notice and pin this up:

Rules: About Nagging

Happy surprises come when you *don't* demand and nag. If you demand more than twice you definitely don't get it.

Proximity and firm intention:

Give one and only one warning.

Go very close to the child. Stare the child directly in the eyes. Keep your face and voice firm, your tone deep and say: 'Second chance'. Then repeat your instruction and wait 3 seconds (count 1, 2, 3, out loud if necessary).

Don't take your children to the supermarket! Especially not at the dangerous crisis time of just before dinner at night!

CONSEQUENCES:

Detach – Do not have eye contact, leave the room.

Distract – Can you help me find your favourite toy?

Defy – Act – 'No treats' for naggers; 'Early bedtime' for persistent demanders.

ACT: If the child has not responded, take some action. Physically remove young children; clap once loudly and say 'Time out' and 'Early bedtime' for older children. Always do what you said you would do and enforce it. Never threaten and not follow through.

COMPASSION: For yourself –keep deep breathing to avoid exploding.

Allow your children to 'make-up' if they want to. Be sure your child heard your instruction, understood it and is physically and emotionally capable of doing the task. Ask why the child is not doing it (but be careful – you may simply be rewarding negative behaviour with attention).

Super-Parent Hot Tip

How to make up:

- Apologise to the person who was upset.
- Tell the person what you will do now to correct the situation.
- Tell the person what you will do in the future.
- State the rule:

e.g. The child would say, 'I'm sorry I hit you. I'll let you play with my Game-boy. Next time I think you took my stuff, I'll ask you about it first. We shouldn't fight'.

EATING PROBLEMS

COPYING: Parents need to model the best behaviour for children to copy: Of course you always eat at the table and use your knife and fork and choose nutritious food... don't you?

CUES: Make the food attractive to look at! Finger food is ideal for young children. Involve older kids in making the shopping list. Keep sweets out of sight. Put small amounts on the plate. Say eat *now or never* and mean it!

CONSEQUENCES: Children will not die if they don't eat everything you want, when you want them to. Say, 'If you don't eat it now, you'll wait until the next appropriate snack or meal time.'

COMPASSION: Some people just hate something – allow 3 'hate items' (e.g. brussel sprouts, spinach, eggs) which children don't have to eat. Admit it, which 3 things do you hate? Give them a choice – e.g. eat your peas *or* pumpkin.

Story

The Problem

Craig, eight years old, had his mother cooking up a storm every night to try to get him to eat. He would pick out one carrot at a time and have to arrange them in order before he chose which one he would eat. Preparation time took ages and then Craig refused to eat it when it was finally ready.

The Solution

The mother told Craig that she would prepare him the same food that the family was to eat. If he didn't eat it, the kitchen was closed until next meal time.

At first Craig cried and whined all night but next day he ate his breakfast!

Super-Parent Hot Tip

The Sweet Treats Jar

Here is a reward strategy to warm the heart of anyone -parents, children and also love partners. It's the Sweet Treats Jar!

What you need to do:

1. Find a large glass jar.

2. Give everyone large squares of coloured paper – a different colour for each participant/family member.

3. Each person makes a list of all the rewarding or positive things they would like to do or have.

4. Each person cuts out small squares of coloured paper and writes one item from their list per square.

5. The paper is then rolled up to look as though it's a coloured sweet and put in the jar. Everybody mixes their colours in the jar so it looks enticingly like a jar of sweets.

6. Each day, one person chooses a coloured sweet (any colour except their own), reads the treat and puts it back in the jar. They then do their utmost to make sure that it actually comes true for that person.

7. Participants are not to ask who gave them a Sweet Treat or what it was. The jar works best if the element of mystery is maintained. This way a halo effect spreads over the family – because you never know who has given you a special treat, so you might as well be nice to everyone!

FIGHTING

COPYING: Parents need to model the best behaviour for children to copy: Ban violent cartoons and movies. Don't let them see *you* watching them.

CUES: Choose a 'Family Warning' word to remind people to calm down, and stop the confrontation. e.g. *danger*.

Say it loudly or whisper it. Display it on the fridge.

CONSEQUENCES: If you didn't see who started it, you'll never find out! so... put them both in the same boat. Say 'People who fight get No Treats and have Early Bedtime'.

COMPASSION: All real injuries need care and attention! If you did see who started it, give the victim a 'special treat'. Detach and Defy the perpetrator and put on No Treats and Early Bedtime and Make-up! Let the culprit know that you still love them, you just don't like their behaviour. If they apologise sincerely from the heart or make a kind gesture they will feel much better.

Story

In one household of six children there was a little miniature armchair. Whoever was in the armchair (which was closest to the television) felt wonderful. They had personal power; they had free space; they had exclusivity; they had uniqueness and . . . they didn't have their vision obscured by somebody else's long legs.

The armchair was so coveted that there was a family rule that if you stood up you had to say '*reserved*'. If you didn't, even the slightest movement away from the chair would find somebody else scrambling in under your nose, firmly sitting down and screaming out in that

RATS!

terrible sing-song 'naa-naa-naa' voice, 'You didn't say RESERVED; you've lost your chair.'

Can you imagine the sense of frustration then? BUT there was no recourse and everyone knew it. The children had made up rules which were working to prevent fights!

Super-Parent Hot Tip

Preventing Fights

At a family meeting, explain to the children that you want to have a fight-free family. Write up a list of the fighting behaviours that are to be stopped and tell them you are going to keep a list. Explain the consequences: that for minor arguing or fighting (example, if the fighting is about a toy or possession) the parent will take the object. When one of the children can quietly and politely tell the parent which child is to have the object you will return it. If the minor fighting is over nothing in particular, you will ignore it. .

Explain that for serious fighting and arguing which is so loud that it disrupts or interferes with other people, you will send all the children to their rooms for ten minutes. For each day that none of the children are caught fighting they will receive a treat.

It may help to nominate one specific area as a fight-free zone. This space will be a haven for parents, of course, but it can also be a quiet space for sick children or someone who has an urgent task (maybe a late piece of homework).

What to do when fighting is dangerous

- Say 'Stop'!!
- Describe what is happening: What you see.

e.g. 'I see two kids who are screaming over what TV station to watch'.

- Say what you feel: 'It makes me angry and fed up'.
- Say 'Fighting to hurt is banned in this family'. Say 'Time Out' and 'Early Bedtime'.

GRANDPARENTS

COPYING: Parents need to model the best behaviour for children to copy: Forgive your parents when they spoil your kids. Remember – if we don't treat our parents well our kids won't be nice to us when we're old!

CUES: Kids are very good at understanding that what's OK at Grandma's is not OK at home. Just make sure that at home, *your* rules are clear and you stick to them. Ask grandparents to at least keep a 'watered-down' version of your rules, e.g. only one TV show, one lolly, one hour to stay up late.

CONSEQUENCES: If grandparents defy you or favour one child over another – have a talk to them, plead and if you get no results... resign yourself to their choices – but keep contact minimal (depending if you need a break or a weekend away) and make it up to the left-out child as best you can!

CHOCOLATE
CHIP
ICECREAM
UNLIMITED!!

COMPASSION: It may be difficult to understand your parents if they completely change their colours – from being tyrants when you were kids, to being totally permissive to your kids, *but* maybe you'll be just like them when it's your turn to be a grandparent?

Kids are very good at seeing context differences and understanding that rules can be different in different situations. For instance, they learn quickly that what they get away with at grandmother's is not acceptable to Mum and not at school!

Super-Parent Hot Tip

STOP fighting about TV watching

The Problem

Are you worried about the way your kids fight about TV? Do your kids watch too much TV? Are you unhappy about the kind of TV that your children watch?

There is a substantial body of evidence to support the negative influence of inappropriate TV watching. During the average child's school life he/she will have seen more than 87,000 acts of violence on TV. Knowing that children learn through *copying*: How parents need to model the best behaviour for children to copy others, don't you agree that TV watching should be carefully screened?

Children are not necessarily able to distinguish between fantasy and reality and their play after watching TV is often aggressive rather than creative or constructive.

The Solution

Read the TV guide and only turn the TV on when there is a suitable program. Teach your child to turn the TV off when the chosen program is finished. Avoid watching any TV in the morning before school. Encourage debate and discussion about programs watched by family members together. Discourage solo TV viewing. Fit TV into your general timetable rather than plan activities around the TV. Keep at least one night of the week TV-free for fun things the family can do together.

HOMEWORK

COPYING: Parents need to model the best behaviour for children to copy: Keep your paperwork a pure experience – do it at a desk, not in front of the TV and get it done on time! Tell your children how good it makes you feel to complete something you were avoiding, like balancing your cheque-book or writing a letter to an overseas friend.

CUES: Everyone has quiet work time before or after dinner at the same time! Make sure each person has a separate and secure work space which is tidy, warm and well-lit.Tape that special TV show to watch later as a reward.

CONSEQUENCES: Rewards for regular homework completion. Give a bonus if it's ahead of time! *No* TV until it's done, *No* food until it's done, *No* $ until it's done.

COMPASSION: Flexibility never hurts... so long as it doesn't result in final last minute pressure, e.g. Allow them to go swimming if it's hot, so long as there is time to do homework the next morning. Be part of their educational experience – even if you weren't the brightest student. Express an interest and nurture their gifts. Encourage a balance between arts and science.

Super-Parent Hot Tips

Timing is everything

Some things parents do inadvertently backfire. For instance, fathers who come home and want to wrestle at 7.00 p.m. can be giving a cue for chaos. Mothers who have worked hard to have the kids calm by this time wring their hands in disbelief at the hectic spree as Dad wrestles with the kids.

Other well-meaning working parents can cause havoc at bedtime. These parents want to make up for not being home all day so they are willing to sit and listen to 'deep and meaningfuls' (d and m reports of upset). And kids are very willing to create 'd and m's' late at night in order to stay up. So avoid the 'd and m's' after 9.00 p.m.

Insistence on homework after 8.00 p.m. can also be a recipe for disaster. It is much more practical to have a cueing system where kids know their homework has to be done by 8.00 p.m. at night. This is suitable for children up to the age of 10. When kids are 10 years or older, homework becomes *their* own problem; so long as they are in their own bedroom and Mum and Dad have quiet space in the house.

Love is letting your children learn by their experiences

Many parents want to protect their children from discomfort. This kind of 'smother love' simply teaches children that their every need will always be met without effort on their part. These kids are demanding and selfish. Do you want your child to be like that?

For children to learn to be responsible for themselves they need to learn (from their own experiences), the kind of consequences that they can expect in the future if they continue that certain behaviour. It's as if they need to be exposed to self-punishment.

If your child has not done her homework, let her explain to the teacher. Then she'll learn that it's up to her! If you do it for her you teach her to rely on you and avoid punishments. If you yell at her, nag her and stand over her while she does it at the last minute, she gets attention (even if it is negative) and learns again to rely on you to prompt her to do 'that homework'.

IGNORING

Easy to say – hard to do

COPYING: Parents need to model the best behaviour for children to copy: Respectful listening is vitally important to healthy relation-ships, *but:*

Ignoring negative behaviours is the best way to handle them.

CUES: Have regular family meetings where everyone takes turns at listening. The person holding the family mascot (a toy selected by your family) speaks – everyone listens!

If *they* ignore you – don't yell, but WHISPER or open a packet of lollies... that'll get their attention!

CONSEQUENCES:

Detach – *is* ignoring. Admittedly, it can be very hard to do in a small house on a rainy day.

Distract – A sudden, sharp noise next to, but not on the ears will certainly get a child's attention and will probably give them a fright too!

If you Deny (say 'No') you are *not* ignoring. Saying *no* may actually reward a child by giving attention!

COMPASSION: Have pity on yourself – You may have to give in *sometimes,* just to get peace!

Super-Parent Hot Tip

Be careful to teach everyone specifically what ignoring looks like. Silence is important but so are your non-verbal behaviours. Don't let the child see your 'fed-up' look. Note that body language is particularly important, silence is important but so are your non-verbal behaviours. Ignoring means no eye contact, deep breathing and calm movements of walking (usually away). Ignoring does not consist of an angry glare, folded arms, frowning eyebrows, clenched fists and jaw.

It is important to be consistent and united. Enrol everyone to react the same way to the naughty behaviour to be ignored. At a family meeting you could role-play how to ignore. Imagine the fun you would have with Dad, for example, playing the part of 'a tantrum terror' and your eight year-old son acting as 'parent' looking in the other direction and not paying the 'naughty child' any attention.

Be a positive parent: programme your child with positives.

Be careful not to cause an accident because of your own fear. Many a child has fallen from a tree or fence and broken a limb because a parent has called out, '*Watch out, you'll fall*!' Immediately after this call, what happens? Yes, the child falls.

Be careful about your language around children. Always have a positive expectation. The brain does not hear a negative. For instance, it doesn't hear 'don't'. Remember what happens when an anxious mother, watching a three-year-old proudly carrying an overfull cup to the table, says, '*Don't spill it*!'

Yes! You're right, of course. The child spills it.

So, instead of warning with a negative line, such as 'Don't get hit by a car!', 'Don't drop it and be messy!' or 'Don't get lost', say it positively; for example: 'You will be careful', 'Take good care'. 'Step carefully'.

JUMPING

COPYING: Parents need to model the best behaviour for children to copy: Walk steady and serenely inside spaces.

CUES: Have an outside jumping spot – use a mini trampoline. Have an obstacle course with jumps outside. Put up a sign inside saying *Walk Zone Only.*

CONSEQUENCES: Reward children who walk calmly inside. People who run inside, immediately go to jump outside for 5 minutes – or do 5 rounds of the obstacle course.

COMPASSION: Bundle everyone up and take kids outside, even on cold rainy days – they need a chance to blow away the cob-webs and let off steam.

Super-Parent Hot tip

A bright idea – the lucky dip prize bag

The lucky dip prize bag is a bag full of inexpensive novelty items. Putting together the lucky dip prize bag can be a lot of fun for everyone. On your next shopping expedition go to a supermarket that stocks an assortment of things. (You might think it's junk, but your kids will love their special 'things'.) Everybody has 5 minutes to go and find 5 things that they would like to have.

Children can have a lucky dip on schedule if promised as a reward or as a surprise, unexpected reward for an especially good effort.

KRAZY, HYPERACTIVE KIDS

COPYING: Parents need to model the best behaviour for children to copy: Practise relaxation and deep breathing regularly – everybody!

CUES: Consult the experts – medical and psychological - to assess diet, health, attention deficit syndrome etc. Have simple, clear rules. Have clear boundaries – physical and behavioural, e.g. Children are banned in dining room unless eating with adults. Shoes are left outside.

Keep them busy and structured

- big motor activities like bike riding only happen outside.
- puzzles and tapes happen inside.

CONSEQUENCES:

Detach: Brief time out – for the child or for you.

Distract: Lay down and deep breathing and listen to a relaxing story tape. Have a warm bath.

Defy: Sharply say 'NO!' and distract.

COMPASSION: Consider everyone. Don't take your 'hyper kids' to the supermarket – why do you think they call them hypermarkets now? Get a kind friend or family member to give you an occasional break and mind your child so that you can have time for you.

Super-Parent Hot Tip

Teaching young children to relax

Parents can encourage an older child to lie down on the bed and read a book for half an hour every afternoon straight after school, as a way of unwinding.

You can try to teach specific relaxation techniques to young children but they get bored easily. Children's imaginations need something to work with, so they much prefer to play the 'Floppy Game' or do 'Magic Breathing' relaxation activities that use the imagination.

THE FLOPPY GAME

The Floppy Game goes like this:

- Imagine that you are becoming loose and floppy. Imagine that your feet can be flip-flapped from side to side and that there is a ripple of rubber stuff that moves all the way up through your legs, into your body, through your neck and into your head.
- The rubbery stuff makes you feel a bit like jelly. All loose and floppy, and you take a great BIG deep breath and you relax and you feel really good, just like a big bowl of jelly, all loose and floppy. You're not going anywhere because the jelly is holding you together.
- You take another deep BIG breath and you are feeling good; relaxed and comfortable.

THE MAGIC BREATHING GAME

- First of all you close your eyes … and you just pat your legs and your tummy and your arms and your head …
- Then you give your head a little massage, just by rubbing gently behind your ears, and you put your arms slowly, slowly by your side and you start to take big deep breaths.
- You breathe with your stomach, so that your stomach moves out and in. Just gently – ever, ever so softly.
- As you breathe you imagine that you have holes in your feet.
- As you breathe in through your nose or your mouth, the air moves all the way down through your body and then out of the holes in your feet.
- Just imagine that the cool air around your nostrils is fresh air and

then the air goes in through your nose or mouth all the way down your body, and comes out as warm, lovely … feet breath!!

- It's like a nice big circle that goes from your feet, up to your head, through your middle and out again.
- You can do 'magic breathing' any time, even in the daytime.
- If you are waiting for someone or if you are a little bit scared, you can do 'magic breathing'.

LAST WORD – 'IT IS'

COPYING: Parents need to model the best behaviour for children to copy: Careful. How often do you have to win 'on principle'? E.g. Did you go to court to dispute that $100 speeding fine?

CUES: Tell them that you will raise your hand and turn your head away when the 'I have to have the last word' intention starts up. Put up a sign on your fridge which reminds everyone to choose to consider others and a happy final outcome:

Do you want to be right? or *Do you want to be happy*?

CONSEQUENCES: Praise patience and understanding.

Detach: Leave the room, refuse to argue – don't be a sparring partner. Ask them for solutions to the problems.Unite against a common enemy. e.g. a grumpy teacher. Acknowledge early that they may be right. Ask questions that have 3 options for answers!

COMPASSION: Never become their enemy. Show you really care for them and don't want them to be upset by the chance they might be wrong, or not have their say.

Story

The Problem

The father was determined to not be like his father who was a dictator and so he allowed his children to feel free to talk back . He wanted his children to be able to challenge someone and to say how they feel. When they crossed that unseen but very real line and became impudent however, a little switch went off inside his brain that said 'No child of mine is going to speak to me that way'.

The Solution

When your child becomes powerful with you, you should not become powerful in return. All you do by trying to exert your power is to lay the foundation for a good knockdown drag-out battle. If you have trouble keeping your temper, you might try leaving the room for a minute or two. This conveys to the child, 'I choose not to fight with you.' A short trip to your bedroom perhaps, and turning the radio on (to drown out the complaints) can allow you to stay in control of your emotions.

MESSY ROOMS

COPYING: Parents need to model the best behaviour for children to copy: Is your bedroom tidy? Do your kitchen cupboards have a system which is kept?

CUES: Put up a checklist (keep extra copies in case it's lost). Help set up storage systems with adequate cupboard space. A little toy box will always overflow and be messy. Have several boxes with different categories. You could colour-code them for big and small toys.

CONSEQUENCES: Praise and reward any attempt to set up systems and keep things tidy.
Untidy room = No treats! Early Bedtime! (if not cleaned by the agreed time).

COMPASSION: Put on a timer and everyone in the family helps to tidy up in a certain time limit, e.g. so they all get an ice-cream.

Super-Parent Hot Tip

Stop the kids from making a mess

Are you fed up and frustrated with the mess that your children make around your home? Are you the only one who ever seems to take responsibility to clean and tidy up? Here's how you can get your kids to keep their personal space and the rest of the house tidy and clean…most of the time… without you having to nag.

It's called *The Silent Robot Box.*

The Silent Robot (a cardboard box) sneaks around once a week and collects up all 'illegal' intruders in the living room or all over the bedroom floor.

Tell the kids that if things are left lying around the house they will be collected and the owner has to wait a whole week to get them back. Every morning you put all stray items in and then hide the box – the boot of your car is a good spot. If the same things are repeatedly left out, you could tell the children they may be asked to donate the items to a worthy cause, seeing they don't seem to value them. Just watch them leap up and put them away then!

NOT LEAVING PARENT
Separation Anxiety

COPYING: Parents need to model the best behaviour for children to copy: Don't linger! Just leave. If you hang around your children will smell your 'guilt' and play on it!

CUES: They know you're going out before you do! They pick up on everything!
Leave security items:

- a photo of you (laminate it, or they'll nibble on it).
- a special toy or blanket.
- Dad's shirt or Mum's scarf (with after-shave or perfume on it).

CONSEQUENCES: Get ear muffs. Enlist the help of a willing supporter.

- With babies aged 7 months – 24 months: Don't sneak! Just go!

- With 2 years up: Practisewith the child 'what you can do if Mummy goes out.'

Set a timer and progressively stay away longer, rewarding after each time the child didn't cry.

COMPASSION: Sorry! You have to be firm! If you give in with this issue, you'll create a noose around your neck and it will be harder to leave next time!
Remember: Short term pain leads to long term gain.

Super-Parent Hot Tip

How to handle the crying baby

Are you exhausted from lack of sleep? Are you at your wits' end about what to do when your baby cries and cries and cries? Many parents have lots of hassles with lack of sleep or interrupted sleep due to their baby's crying. How do you know when to go to your crying baby?

Here's the solution: follow aunty's rule which says: If baby cries for more than 20 minutes, there is something wrong and you had best go check. Maybe it's sore gums, colic or a full nappy.

Because babies can't communicate their needs, it's up to busy parents to anticipate or deal with disasters. Let's face it – would you stop crying if you had a smelly mess in your knickers?

With experience, you may be able to tell the difference between a real distress cry and a tantrum cry.

With consistency, persistency and a set of ear muffs to last out the 20 minutes wait, you may even get a good night's sleep.

OPEN COMMUNICATION

COPYING: Parents need to model the best behaviour for children to copy: Be available and be a good listener. Make quality time a priority for your children. Share some of your upsets, fears and weaknesses.

CUES: Find 5 minute 'special' times each day.

1. After the morning rush dies down.
2. After dinner.
3. In the bath.

Use open-ended questions. Not – 'Was school good today?' but – 'Tell me some good things that have happened today.'

CONSEQUENCES: Have 'Loving Days.'

e.g. Mummy or Daddy's Day – parent takes kids somewhere special or kids take parents to their special place.

The major consequence of poor communication is that a person feels invalidated. The parent should ask, 'Did the child feel listened to? Was the child talked at, or talked with?'

COMPASSION: Just love. Just love with happy hearts.

Super-Parent Hot Tip

Coping with teenagers and peer pressure

The Problem

Are you fed up and frustrated with your teenagers' behaviour? Do they swear, eat junk food, watch TV all the time, and seem to really enjoy doing nothing? If you say something is black – do they say it's white? Do they listen to their peers' opinions and reject yours?

The Solution

Don't fight with your teenagers about the influence of peer pressure. Understand that their greatest need is to be accepted by their peers and not rejected. Teens need parents to be good listeners who encourage open honest communication and are sensitive to their feelings –especially about wanting to be part of the in crowd.

Give them the space to make mistakes when they follow their peers and don't rub their noses in them. Gradually give your teens the independence they crave and praise them for all the times they do act responsibly. Believe that ultimately they do share your values and will live by them.

PERFECTIONISM

COPYING: Parents need to model the best behaviour for children to copy: Be willing to admit your own mistakes and allow for human error to be OK. Teach your children that we often learn more from our mistakes. Express your feelings honestly. Learn how to accept a compliment. Have you ever caught yourself saying, 'Oh this old thing.' That's a put down to yourself and to the person who complimented you. Watch out because your children will learn how to do that from you.

CUES: Practise timed events where it's impossible to get an item finished and praise the efforts more than the results. Encourage a 'daggy' day – a day for dressing for pleasure rather than to please others. Adopt a 'that will have to do' attitude to avoid obsessing about annoyances which can't be fixed. Eg. A pimple on your chin or, hair that sticks up.

CONSEQUENCES: Relaxation and deep breathing. Imagine coping with the worst. Teach coping self-talk, e.g. It doesn't matter if I don't come first at Little Athletics, so long as I do my personal best. I'll aim to beat my personal best next time.

COMPASSION: Say: It's not how many goals you get, but how you play the game that counts.

Super-Parent Hot Tip About Self-Esteem

There are three main aspects of self-esteem.

1. Feeling Capable. Children need to feel capable to feel that they have power over their environment and that they can do things to change it.

2. Feeling Connected. Children need to know they belong to their family, their school and the broader community. They need to feel included and know that: 'Hey, I belong here and in my world we share these values and beliefs'.

3. Feeling Worthwhile. Every child needs to feel unique and special and unconditionally lovable. They need to know that regardless of what they do, they are an individual who is a worthwhile human being. They are OK!

Good self-esteem doesn't rely on consistent successes. We can't and shouldn't try to protect our children from upsets and learning experiences; in fact they grow in maturity and in self-esteem when they know they've put in their best effort even if they didn't succeed in the eyes of the external world.

That's what children have to be taught by their parents. How to acknowledge themselves for their best efforts, even if they don't succeed compared to some external standard. Because after all how do we ever know if we were successful in the eyes of the external world? Is it when we were on top of the heap? But compared to who?

The most useful definition of success is, 'putting in your best effort and getting results that you feel good about'. They don't have to be excellent, and they don't even have to pass. Even if it is a learning experience, so long as you did learn from it and you're happy that you did your best shot, then you know you've had a success.

That's certainly what I want my children to do: 'Give things their best shot.'

What do you want for your children?

QUESTIONS

COPYING: Parents need to model the best behaviour for children to copy: It's good to ask questions, to have an inquisitive and curious mind, *but* sometimes questions are not welcome.

CUES: Tell the child: 'I'll raise my hand in the air and turn my head away if you keep asking questions that I'm unable to cope with'.

CONSEQUENCES: Praise self control: 'It's good to see you thinking over the many answers to that question. You've got a good mind.'

Counter with another question; 'What do you think?' or 'Could you ask your father/teacher that ?'

Say 'I just don't know. Let's find out together' (make a time to go to library, zoo or look it up on the internet).

COMPASSION: Keep your sense of humour. You may have been that child who always asked 'how' or 'why' when you were little.

Super-Parent Hot Tip

Praise the effort and don't put the child down

Another crucial strategy for a parent to be awareof is to avoid putting your child down. For example, when little Mr Four is proudly showing his mother his first attempts at making his bed he says, 'Look Mummy, I did it mine own self'. He is very sad when his mum just frowns and says, 'That's not good enough. You don't make a bed like that. Watch me and I'll show you how to make a bed properly.'

What he needs is praise. 'That's a terrific job for a big four year old. Well done!'

WHY? WHY?
WHY? WHY? WHY?
WHY? WHY? WHY?
WHY? WHY? WHY?
WHY? WHY? WHY?
WHY?
WHY? WHY? WHY? WHY?
WHY?
WHY? WHY? WHY?
WHY? WHY?
WHY? WHY? WHY?

RAMPANT LIES, TELLING TALES AND DOBBING

COPYING: Parents need to model the best behaviour for children to copy: Do you always tell the truth? E.g. is the cheque really in the mail?

CUES: Keep valuables safely secured – don't tempt! NO favouritism – it can lead to jealousy. Discuss the effect on others – comment on the moral (how not telling the truth causes disasters for everyone) in stories and movies.

CONSEQUENCES: Reward honesty and positive behaviour with approval and thanks. Make the punishment fit the crime. 'Make up' to the injured party by saying sorry and doing something to help. Let children know that if they tell the truth from the beginning, the punishment won't be so bad. E.g. If they broke your family heirloom vase and they admit it, temper your response. You may be livid, but they were honest and are more likely to come to you in the future, knowing they can trust your judgment and you will keep your word to them that you won't 'over-react'.

COMPASSION: Understand that children often do not truly know the difference between fantasy and reality. Be open and forgiving so kids can trust you.

Super-Parent Hot Tip

Telling tales

Small children are particularly good at telling tales and parents often fall into the trap of inconsistently rewarding tale telling with attention.

Some parents refuse to allow any 'tale telling' or 'dobbing'. There is a problem, however, when something really dangerous happens or seems likely to happen and you may have discouraged your children to the point where it is not reported. So instead of banning 'dobbing' altogether it could be useful to listen to a very brief report. If you find that a situation is not dangerous, be respectful, acknowledge the child's feelings, then encourage them to go off and find their own solution. If it's dangerous, ACT.

The dobbing book

An innovative idea is to give each child a special exercise book in which they can create long lists of all the mean horrible things that other siblings do to them. This is called the dobbing book and if necessary it can be brought to family meetings and (if appropriate) can be discussed.

SHARING and TAKING TURNS

COPYING: Parents need to model the best behaviour for children to copy: Sharing is a universal problem, adults go to court over it and countries go to war over it. Be a good sharer yourself, demonstrate sharing with the people around you so your child will want to model from you.

CUES: Give them responsibility. Encourage but don't make them share or they might resent you. Invite your children to share. Point out the advantages of sharing to them.

Encouraging taking turns and sharing really can be a formidable task in any family because we live in such close confines. How do we draw our limits or boundaries? This is more of a problem in small homes where children have to share bedrooms and adults have to share leisure/living space with children. Why do so many homes, no matter how financially placed, often have two or more TV sets? Unfortunately, the obvious answer is that it avoids fights.

CONSEQUENCES: TV soapies show the children drawing co-operatively on the kitchen table and sharing their paints and pastels. Suzie says, 'Here Joe, you can have my favourite gold texta now' and Joe says, 'Oh, thank you'. In real life, Joe might sneak Suzie's gold texta behind her back. A very tense Suzie on discovering her missing texta, screams, 'Give me back my texta, you pig'. If Joe feels kindly he might, at best, throw it at her without hitting her on the head.

Reward all attempts to share. Praise abundantly!

To encourage sharing, parents need to be ever aware of any positive co-operation between their kids and to praise heavily. Praise both children even if only one is giving and the other receiving, so that the receiver feels good and wants to reciprocate later. Make co-operation

reports a highlight of family meetings and celebrate them hugely – hoot and clap and smile and laugh. Sharing is a great way to feel bonded as a team.

COMPASSION: A major influence on willingness to share is how the other person responds. Have you ever offered someone something very precious to you and been rebuffed by their offhand refusal? Did you feel invalidated? Did you feel like sharing with that person again? To help encourage sharing, you could talk at a family meeting about accepting things with grace. Helping others save face. You probably do this very well yourself – parents are constantly having to put up with offers of help from wee ones who want to help in the kitchen, the garden or just 'hop into bed' with us so we don't feel lonely. Watch for every opportunity to reward the behaviours that you want. If a child requests a turn, you could say, 'I was so proud of how nicely you asked for your turn.'

Super-Parent Hot Tip

At family meetings, practise:

- How to offer to share
- How to respond in a positive way to sharing offers from other children
- How to ask for a turn appropriately
- How to respond in a positive way to requests for a turn
- How to let others share
- How to respond positively when another person lets you share.

Reality of sharing

In my days as a school psychologist I used to go into many school staffrooms and I was struck by a common problem – nobody washed their cups, or people fiercely guarded their own cups with their special name and hook. Visitors had to find the best leftover cups from a few very old and dusty cups in the back of a cupboard. I'm sure it is the same in most organisations.

In the light of this model of human nature, is it any wonder that kids have problems taking turns and sharing? They just naturally do not see it as a desirable value. Saying, 'it's mine' feels so good (just say it out aloud right now and remember how good it felt when you were a child). Childhood is an egocentric developmental stage, so it's amazing that children comply with adult imposed standards at all.

TANTRUMS

COPYING: Parents need to model the best behaviour for children to copy: Can you stay calm when you miss out on the weekly Lotto draw by just one number?

CUES: Are they tired, sick, confused, jealous? Don't promise you'll buy them something later. When you go out shopping they'll want it NOW! Kids couldn't care less when and where they have tantrums, in fact a reallyclever kid will learn that public put down and humiliations for parents can get a lot more mileage than the private ones.

Some kids have tantrums to get power, revenge, attention or even just to opt out, sometimes they're for manipulation and sometimes they are just genuine tantrums where the child is overwhelmed by stimulation, tired, sick or even scared.

CONSEQUENCES:

Toddlers

Detach – leave the room
Distract – Read a story
Defy – Say no, put the child in Time Out*

Older Children

All the above plus encourage them to recognise their own 'symptoms' and avoid them by deep breathing, and listening to a relaxation audiotape/cd, or doing ten star jumps to release the tension.

COMPASSION:

The only person to have compassion for a child in full tantrum-mode is that interfering grandmother type in the supermarket who wants to give them the lollypop you said NO to! Detach from her and say NO to ensure that she doesn't get away with it.

* Listen to the audiotape/cd entitled *Easy Tantrum Taming by* Dr Janet Hall for a clear, step-by-step procedure for handling and defusing tantrums.

Super-Parent Hot Tip

First ask yourself, why is the tantrum happening?

The answer is because it works of course! It gets attention, a reaction. For some children, negative attention is better than no attention at all. A tantrum can also be a convenient distraction; to avoid a chore or to cover up a greater sin like not doing homework.

Second, ask what's the solution?

It's important to be consistent so that everyone reacts the same way to a tantrum – *ignore it.*

Watch out for the biggest pitfall – falling into the trap of taking the bait when the angry parent ends up fighting with the child. The calm parent needs to say, 'I'm not buying into that' – and *ignore* the tantrum!

Why do young children tantrum so much?

It's part of their knee-jerk reaction to the frustration of not getting what they want, when they want. And it generally makes them feel better to express their frustrations by having a tantrum. A young child doesn't have the ability to rationalise and reason like a mature young person or adult, so they go into a tantrum as stress release.

Young children are learning at a phenomenal rate. In fact they learn 50 per cent of their lifetime learning in the first four years of their life. That's a hectic pace. If we were facing that kind of learning curve we'd probably go into tantrum mode too!

Toddlers live only in the present, therefore if they want something and they want it *now*, it's because *now* is the only time there is. They don't understand what 'later' is and they have no skills and strategies for coping with the frustration of waiting.

STAY CALM.
IGNORE
TRANTRUMS!

UPSET

COPYING: Parents need to model the best behaviour for children to copy: Don't be a cold, wet fish! If you are upset, show your feelings if appropriate (especially you Dads).

CUES: Be careful to prevent scary things from happening to your child – drive safely, put sharp and poisonous things away, don't watch scary movies at night, keep happy things happening.

CONSEQUENCES: Allow the upset to be expressed but put a time limit on it! If you are angry – limit it to 20 minutes and then 'toss it over your shoulder' and move on. Don't lay down on a weeping child's bed! Encourage children to independently remover themselves from upset and use positive self-talk: e.g. Soothe yourself and say 'I'm upset I didn't make the team but I'll work harder on my batting so next time I'm picked.'

COMPASSION: Tears are the rainbow of the Soul. Cry together and make it OK especially for little boys to cry.

Super-Parent Hot Tip

Routine for coping with Upsets

Routines and rituals can be really very reassuring and give a sense of security and safety. Young children can become very dependent on dummies and security blankets. While this can be extremely frustrating for a family when the loved object gets left behind, children deserve to have their special symbol of reassurance close to them at all times.

If desperate, you can always tell your troubles to the 'Worry Dolls'. In Guatemala the natives make tiny dolls as big as your fingernail which live in a little wooden patterned box. Before you go to bed each night, you tell each doll one of your worries and pop it in the box. When the dolls are in the box you put the lid on and go to sleep. During the night the dolls take care of your problems, so the next day when you wake up you can be happy and relaxed, knowing that your problems are being dealt with. You can buy Guatemalan dolls in many retail stores, or you could make your own – maybe with your child. What a good reason to share some fun, quality time! Probably you'll enjoy telling the dolls your worries too, so you can get a good night's sleep.

Super-Parent Hot Tip

How to help kids cope with upsets

There are four steps parents can follow to help kids cope with and handle upsets. It's easy to remember these steps as the four 'W's' :

1.What happened? 2. What if? 3. Wants and wishes 4. Why not?

Notice that in 'What happened', it's important to acknowledge and reflect the bad feelings involved. Don't avoid expression of negative feelings as this can actually result in more upset and fighting.

1. **Show that you know what happened and understand their feelings: describe *what happened*?**

The parent says: 'He took your book and you're mad at him'.

2. **Show that you appreciate how important it is to him and point out the *what if's*?**: The parent says: 'What if you did that to him? How would he like it? What if you wrecked all of his good stuff?'

3. **Show that you understand what is wanted – *wants* and *wishes*:**

The parent says 'You want him to respect your things. I bet you wish he'd ask before he took something of yours.'

4. **Help come up with preventive solutions – *why not*?**

The parent says 'Why not tell him to:

- leave your things alone.
- knock on your door before coming in to your room.
- stay out of your room if the door is shut'.

VOMITING

COPYING: Parents need to model the best behaviour for children to copy: No-one likes vomiting but it's an unfortunate part of life, especially with small children (and what goes down their gullets!)... so be matter of fact about it all!

CUES: Careful of the 'junk food', the birthday party overload, the virus going around crèche and don't let them wear white!

CONSEQUENCES:

When kids say 'I want a bucket', get the bucket...*fast*!

COMPASSION: Heaving tummies hurt! Understand that some children are actually phobic about the thought of vomiting so be aware of how much special love they need.

Super-Parent Hot Tip

Drawings

Everyone has a natural ability to express feelings through images and many of us can actually draw well. (At least you lucky adults who didn't have a mean teacher criticise your drawings can probably still draw!) Encourage your child to draw her most scary thought about vomiting.

You may then be able to empathise with just how real and how powerfully scary her fears are. Then it's time to help the child to express her own power over the fear. Ideas include:

- Burn the scary picture.
- Cut it into pieces and scatter them in the wind or over a cliff or flush them down the toilet.
- Tip paint or nail polish over it.
- Draw it over and over again, but getting smaller each time, until it disappears!

Sleep therapy

A wonderful strategy for parents who have been concerned about their children's night terrors or general daytime anxiety is to use the sleep therapy technique. With sleep therapy the parent goes into the room during the night (perhaps just before the parent goes to sleep) and stands very quietly beside the bed, looking at the sleeping child.

The beauty of the sleeping child never fails to amaze! What love and joy fills the parent's heart. Gone completely is the upset of the daytime tantrums and emotional dramas. There is nothing but love in the space between sleeping child and watching parent.

A really good strategy is for the parent to match his breathing with the child's breathing. The parent then says the child's name and just touches the child very gently on the face. The parent then waits and, usually, the child will stir ever so slightly. The parent then says the sleep therapy affirmation.

The sleep therapy affirmation

You are a beautiful, beautiful child .... (Put in your child's name.)

Mummy and Daddy love you very much.

Sleep easy, sleep well – tomorrow will be a beautiful day.

I love you.

The parent then leaves the room very quietly.

Amazingly positive things can happen the next day as both child and parent carry in their hearts an unconscious memory of the connection that they made in the middle of the night.

WORRYING

COPYING: Parents need to model the best behaviour for children to copy: Most people spend a substantial amount of time worrying about things that never happen! Be a good model! Don't worry! Be happy!

CUES: Children need to feel safe and know what to expect. Tell stories about others who overcome their fears! Keep a reassuring, routine life-style. Exercise together – tired bodies are too exhausted to worry.

CONSEQUENCES: Reward confident behaviour. Be a good listener but don't overdo it! *No* deep and meaningful discussions at night. Use the power of the imagination to kill that worry! Draw it and flush it down the toilet.

NB. A pet can soothe a worried child.

COMPASSION: Honour the worry and then turn it into a positive. e.g. a rainy day may spoil an excursion but then we can stay inside and do drawings or dress-ups.

Super-Parent Hot Tip

The reward of attention

The psychological principle of reward says that if a consequence increases the likelihood that a behaviour will occur again, then that consequence must be a reward. If a child cries at night, for example, and the mother comes into the room and spends some time being loving and asking the child all about her concerns, the mother is rewarding the crying behaviour. Crying may recur the next night in the hope that the same attention will be received.

I know that this is very hard for some parents to face. You believe that you are doing the best thing to go to a crying child, and certainly if the child has genuine fear, he deserves to have some support and affection ... but it is a Catch 22 situation! How does a parent know when it is a case of genuine fear or when the child is playing on the drama?

Because it is very difficult to be really sure, it is probably best to offer the child some verbal reassurance and arrange all the 'security-blanket' props needed for the child to go to sleep. Spend as short a time as possible doing this and arrange to talk about it again the next morning.

Teach your child the power of positive self-talk

One of the most powerful ways in which fear is maintained is the negative self-talk that the child runs in his mind. A fearful child's internal self-talk is saying 'Something is dangerous and will hurt me. I must avoid being near it at all costs. Being near it is awful and I can't bear to even think about it. I can't cope'.

The child needs to learn the antidote to this negative self-talk – talking positively instead!

Positive self-talk is a very important skill for coping with fear or anxiety. You can use self-talk to program yourself to expect a positive outcome for a situation that could otherwise be scary.

Coping self-talk moves through four stages:

1. Fear-alert: ask yourself 'what exactly is scary?'
2. Counter-defence: ask 'what is true and rational?'
3. Positives: ask 'what is positive and easy?'
4. Self-reward: congratulate yourself for coping.

For example: A child who has to present a talk in front of a class could use self-talk in this way:

1. 'I'm going to be good today when I do my talk.'
2. 'It is only to my teacher, who I know very well, and all my class friends really do want me to do well.'
3. 'I really enjoyed all their talks. It is going to be very easy and I am going to enjoy it.'
4. 'I am a good presenter.'

Caution: Teach your child that it's best to use self-talk very softly or under your breath – some people might think you are a bit strange if they hear you doing it loudly!

* For more information on helping scared and worried children, see Dr Janet Hall's book – *Fear-free Children*.

 ASPERATED PARENTS

COPYING: Parents need to model the best behaviour for children to copy: Look around next time you're out (exasperated parents are everywhere and they usually give in or explode!). Don't be like them (if you can help it!). Stop and calm down – calmness is contagious.

CUES: The myth of the 'Perfect Parent' – don't believe it.
For children who set up their parents, 'But Mummy/Daddy said I could!' ... don't believe it. Check with your partner first.

CUES: (to avoid) Overload at work or home. Money blues. PMT Supreme. A deadline to meet which makes you anxious.

CONSEQUENCES: Give each other a break – Mum's/Dad's night out! Learn to do deep breathing and relax. Throw spit balls into a bucket from close range. Go to the gym and exercise or run around the block. Have a 'parent sanctuary' in your house – kid proofed of course – play loud music! Hibernate in the toilet or in the car. See a family therapist. Have a nanny for the day.

COMPASSION: Remember *Short-term pain* leads to *Long-term gain*. Parent determination must be greater than parent guilt.

COMPASSION: Congratulate yourself! You're a parent – you have the most responsible job in the whole world – *and* you are doing the best you can!

Super-Parent Hot Tip

Parent stress

Children can feel their parents' tension. Be careful to manage your own upsets with stress management techniques such as exercise, meditation and deep breathing.

Overtiredness. Let's face it, even adults can get grumpy and irritable when we're overtired. Children who are difficult in the evening may be simply saying 'I need my bed.'

Hints to help parents to sleep

Keep sleep a pure experience. Keep your bedroom just for sleep.

- do not keep a TV in your bedroom
- read sitting up, in a chair
- make love outside of the bed!

Don't fall asleep in front of the television (If your children copy you it will be a lifetime problem for them).

YELLING & HITTING

COPYING: Parents need to model the best behaviour for children to copy: There's a classic cartoon of a father spanking his son across his knee, saying; 'I'll teach you not to hit your brother!' Oh dear, not good copying behaviour. If you hit and yell, your child learns to hit and yell and possibly will do it even better than you!

CUES: Come up close to warn them to stop – you don't need to yell if you can see the whites of their eyes! Keep your hands under your armpits. We all need to let off steam sometimes – yell into a pillow and punch it. Do this together and then laugh together.

CONSEQUENCES: Praise and reward patience, co-operation and quiet negotiation.

Detach – leave the room.

Distract – let's do aerobic exercises! Put on loud rock and roll music.

Defy – a loud noise close to an ear (but not on it) e.g. snap fingers.

COMPASSION: Rescue the victim and make a big fuss. Speak with calm intention to be clear and have the other person understand.

Mean things people say to each other.

Every family member has a hot button – something somebody else knows they can say, which will make the other person's blood boil. Have a look at the list of typical things kids say to each other to be mean. Notice the warning – These words are toxic and should be banned! Unfortunately, I'm sure that many readers of this book would be able to report lots of other mean words kids say to kids, not to mention the frightful things they say to their parents . . . like 'I wish I was adopted'! Your hot button might be pushed by a simple, 'Are you dumb or something?' Or it might go off when you hear that absolutely foul XXXX word. You know, that one. The one you don't like hearing. Whatever it is, you can be sure it's going to be said in the middle of a family fight. Family members know exactly how to hurt each other – at our weakest point.

For example:

Mum arrives late to collect 9-year old son from sport. 'You never remember to pick me up', he screams. 'You probably won't be on time next time, you never are', he screams louder. 'You always get there on time for her' (sister). 'You love her more than me. Don't you?'

<u>Mean things kids say to hurt each other</u>

No one loves you. You're fat/ugly/skinny/dumb/stupid. You've got funny eyes/legs/pimples/ears etc. You don't belong in this family. You're useless/hopeless. Who'd sit next to you?. You stink. You're a nothing. Mum and Dad like me better than you. Did you just escape from a lunatic farm? I hate you. You're an idiot.

Super-Parent Hot Tip

<u>Made-up stories</u>

Parents and children can learn a lot about how to prevent and manage frustrations and 'being naughty' and yelling and hitting by telling real-life or made-up stories themselves. In our family we used to spend a lot of time travelling and the children would ask us to tell them a story. We used to choose a problem such as lighting fires, stealing or being taken away by a stranger and base a story on the particular problem. One storyline was about girls who were clever and silly girls who got into trouble.

Silly/Clever story:

The silly girl talked to a stranger in the street and got into his car. She was taken away and badly hurt. The clever girl told the stranger to go to the police station if he wanted directions, and she ran to the nearest safety house.

The silly girl got the matches, lit a fire and burned the house down. The clever girl took the matches from the baby and then told her mother.

Sometimes these stories went on and on, with more and more detail. The moral was always simple and sweet! Parents make up a story about a situation very like their own child's. The parent tells a story depicting the child's worry or concern and adds a wonderfully successful twist at the end in which the child overcomes her problem.

Making up your own stories is a lot of fun and children really learn by making up possible outcomes for their own or parents' stories.

Ideas for stories

What stories could you make up? First set the scene, then talk through how children would cope with problems. Give them lots of ideas about practical and imaginary things that they could do.

For example:

What would happen if ...

- Imagine if you came home one day and found that Mum and Dad weren't in the house?
- What if we had been called away unexpectedly, or what if we had got stuck in traffic after there had been a very bad accident and couldn't get through the traffic?
- Or what if one of us had broken a leg?

Of course, don't end the story until you have arrived at a positive outcome.

Zzzzz... Sleeping problems and bedtime battles

SLEEP PROBLEMS*

Not able to get to sleep. Not able to stay in own room. Nightmares and night terrors.

COPYING: Parents need to model the best behaviour for children to copy: Do you fall asleep in front of the TV?

CUES: Wind-down before bed time – *no wrestles with dad!* Have a checklist – toileted, fed and watered, story, soft toy etc. Use a Mummy and Dad audiotape/ cd with reassuring sounds, kisses and... yawns. Drink warm milk. Watch the Monsters Inc Disney cartoon where the monsters are scared of children! Have a monster toy that the child takes to bed to scare off the other monsters.

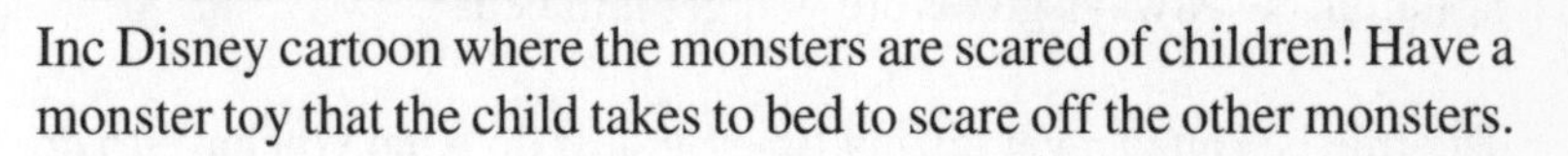

CONSEQUENCES: Scared children sometimes need comforters** (something with Mum or Dad's smell, security blanket). Encourage the child's imagination to scare away the monsters. Do a 'monster check' in the cupboard and under the bed to reassure the child that no monster could be hiding in their bedroom.

COMPASSION: Nightmares and night terrors need cuddles and warm reassurance.

* For other sleep problems (child gets up-stays up etc.)

see: *How You Can Be Boss of Bedtime*. By Dr Janet Hall.

** For scared kids see the section *How You Can Be Boss of Burglars, Bogeymen and Big Black Dogs* in the book *Fear-free Children* by Dr Janet Hall.

HOW TO COUNTERACT/ANTICIPATE BEDTIME DE-LAYING TACTICS

Prerequisite: Child has own bed-time checklist pinned behind bedroom door.

The standard rule is: You can get up any time to go to the toilet, or get a drink or whatever. You don't have to tell your parents but you have to go straight back to bed.

Problem:	Asking for a drink.
Solution:	Pre-bed arrangement, child gets own drink ready and has it in the bedroom at hand.
Problem:	Child needs to go to the toilet.
Solution:	Always go before you get into bed.

The rule is: You can get up any time but just do what you have to do (e.g. Get a drink, go to the toilet), you don't have to tell your parents.

Practise going to the toilet (Parents may need to supervise 'dark time' practice while the child is getting out of bed and walking to the toilet in the dark.)

Have a torch ready. Count how many steps it is. Sing a song all the way from the bed to the toilet and back again. Have a night light ready if necessary. Make sure the child can get his or her own blankets back on again easily and settle down in bed.)

If desperate have a potty underneath the bed. And... you might like to make sure older children understand that they have to be responsible for cleaning the potty in the morning.

Problem: Crying out for parents.

Solution: Tell the child that all crying out will be ignored.

You must absolutely stick to your guns – do not go to the child under any circumstances.

WARNING: Reward the child for going through a whole night without crying out.

Problem: 'I need a story'

Solution: Have a selection of stories that children can read themselves. Even younger children can have picture stories without words.

For example there are two books by Jan Ormerod called *Sunshine* and *Moonshine* which depict family morning and night routines. Also, you could have an audiotape/cd as a substitute for a story.

Note: A story read by Mum and Dad can always be a special time activity. But bedtime stories need to be limited to one short, pre-selected story, read as a reward for being snug in bed, on time.

Problem : 'I need a kiss'

Solution : Make sure you give the child a kiss when you tuck him or her in.

Tell them, 'this is your good-night kiss.' Get them to say, 'Yes, that's my good-night kiss' (to put it on record they just got one!) Then there are no complaints that 'you didn't give me a kiss.' The parent could also plant a kiss on the child's favourite toy in bed with them and say, 'if you need a kiss, you can get this one from the golliwog.'

<u>Problem</u>: Child needing special toy (and only *that* special toy).

<u>Solution</u>: Store that special toy in the same place all the time. Have a duplicate special toy hidden in the parents' cupboard. Make sure the special toy is in the bed before you say goodnight.

A very tired father told how junior was happy left with relatives way over the other side of town at 10.00 a.m. in the morning. At 10.00 p.m. things were not so happy when Junior had been crying for 2 hours because he had no teddy. Dad drove all the way over town with teddy and when he finally arrived, found that Junior had fallen into an exhausted sleep, just 5 minutes before!

<u>Problem</u>: My toy needs a love from you.

<u>Solution</u>: The Magic Love Heart. Make a love heart picture, cover it in plastic and leave it with the child.

Tell the child, this love heart is a magic love heart from me to you. It will always provide you with all the love that you, your toys, their imaginary friends and any other presence in your bedroom would need throughout the night. This love heart is a force which can keep them safe from anything.

<u>Problem</u>: The room needs tidying.

<u>Solution</u>: Have a rule: No tidying up after bedtime.

<u>Problem</u>: 'I forgot to do my homework'.

<u>Solution</u>: Set the alarm for an hour earlier than usual get up time. It is the child's responsibility to wake and complete homework. If not, then the child has to explain it to the teacher.

Problem: 'I need a costume for a special dress up day at school tomorrow'.

Solution: This is a tricky one – if possible, hire it on the way (or ring up Grandma or another family supporter and delegate the problem.) Same thing for a cake needed for the next day.

Problem: There is something very serious and important that I have to tell you.

Solution: Make an agreement to talk to the child about it first thing the morning.

WARNING:This postponement will only work if you :

- Can be trusted to keep your appointment.
- Have *already* given the child an opportunity earlier in the evening – at dinner, or bath time or in the 'Good Night Sleep Right Sleep Tight' game, to share that serious and 'Oh so important' thing they need to tell you.

Never have a deep and meaningful discussion with a child late at night.

Few problems are ever solved at night. Does this sound familiar? Husband and wife lay in bed until 3.00 a.m. having a serious talk about their marriage being over. Next morning in the light of the day, they can't imagine why they ever thought there was anything wrong with the marriage.

If your child has something serious to discuss with you, it can wait until the morning. *Don't feel guilty*!

But do keep the agreement when you make an appointment and make sure that you allocate time for it in the morning.

PROBLEMS WITH CHILDREN WHO GET INTO THEIR PARENTS' BED AT NIGHT

Parents who let their children into their bed at night create a rod for their own back. Unfortunately, the first time they do it is probably for a very good reason. Imagine the typical scenario:

A very, very, exhausted parent sound asleep in the dead of night is awakened by a weeping, distressed child. The parent gets out of bed, takes the child back, tucks them in, gets them a drink of water, sings them a song, soothers them down, staggers back to bed and is flat on their back, out like a light, snoring soundly – for five minutes.

Do you know what it feels like lying in bed, sealing your eyes tight with disbelief. This time there is no crying distressed child, but you know that they are there. You know the feeling of being in bed and just feeling somebody in the space? You can feel their breathing. You have an internal fight with yourself. Don't open your eyes, don't open your eyes. Finally it gets to you. You open your eyes and the child begins to cry.

Same old set up!

Is it any wonder that eventually you give in and let the child crawl into your bed? At least that way you get to have the sleep that you sorely need. What is the solution?

Make a very clear rule with yourself and stick to it. The child is *not allowed* in your bed. It is much harder to get a child out of a parent's bed than it is for a parent to get out of a child's bed. If you genuinely have a very traumatic period where your child must sleep with you, you go and sleep in their bed. Mind you this is only a last resort.

So what can parents do about children getting into their bed at night?

Put them back into their own beds in their own bedrooms.

Do it from the very beginning.

Do it consistently.

Do it without showing the child any affection, warmth or emotional reaction and insist that they stay in their own bed at night.

MY SUPER PARENTS!

ACCELERATED SUCCESS CENTRE

DR JANET HALL'S BOOKS AND TAPES

Available through: Save Secretarial Service PO Box 5000 Middle Camberwell 3124

Phone: [03] 9888 6522 or Email: jrichard@bigpond.net.au

WANT TO LEARN MORE FROM DR JANET HALL?

Dr Janet Hall has a uniquely user-friendly way of delivering information. She talks directly to you in everyday, easy to understand terms so that you get maximum benefit in applying her suggested ideas and strategies directly into your life to achieve the success that you deserve.

All of Jan's information is readily attainable by contacting her directly :

1. Through her email address: info@drjanethall.com.au and
2. Through her websites: www.goalmaker.com
   www.drjanethall.com.au
   www.bedwetting.com.au
   www.sex-therapy.com.au

FAMILY BOOKS BY DR JANET HALL

Fear-free Children

A book which provides a unique insight into the causes, symptoms and treatment of problem fears in children**, Fear-free Children** shows how fears can be overcome with confidence-building activities, games, stories, self-talk and rewards. **Fear-free Children** is written in two sections – the first giving information for parents and the second teaching examples through stories for younger children. Teenagers can benefit from reading the entire book and directly applying the information to their own circumstance.

The simplicity makes it easy to understand, adapt and apply so that you quickly get control over your fears and learn to solve your own problems.

Fight-free Families

Did you know that 85 per cent of families have had their first fight before 9 a.m. in the morning?

And they often fight at dinner and especially before bed! **Fight-free Families** explains why people fight and gives terrific ideas for how to manage fights, but even better – avoid them. It is possible to have an (almost) fight-free family by creating an environment at home that supports the peaceful resolution of conflict.

How You Can Be Boss of Bedtime

Here is an effective solution for all parents who feel frustrated and fed up when children's bedtime arrives. This book promotes a win-win situation which empowers children to actively plan and participate in their own bedtime routine. The first section of the book is designed for children to read or for it to be read to them. The second section of the book provides parents with information on sleep behaviours and details success strategies which work wonders.

How You Can Be Boss of the Bladder

Dr Janet Hall is the founder of the Boss of The Bladder Program in Melbourne, Australia.This book is designed to help both children and parents gain some insight into the management and eventual control of day- and night-wetting.

Children read the first section and are relieved to find out that it's not them who wets on purpose – it's that pesky 'bladder muscle'. Parents are coached in realistic prevention, management and even cure strategies for bedwetting. Everybody boosts their self-esteem when children get dry!

Easy Toilet Training

You will learn the easy procedure for effective toilet training which doesn't make you pull your hair out. You get up-to-date knowledge on the essential steps of toilet training which include timing, readiness and personality differences.

Easy Toilet Training gives step-by-step procedures for effective toilet training with maximum ease and fun for all! After reading this book you will know how to get results quickly, with the least effort and without hiccups.

SexWise: What every YOUNG PERSON and Parent Should Know About Sex

This book enrols teenagers in a commitment to responsible sex – choosing the right person, age, place, time, safety and all for the right reasons.

SexWise is a wonderful book for parents because it does all their hard work and saves embarrassment!

GOOD PARENTING AUDIOTAPES BY DR JANET HALL

How To Super-Boost Your Child's Self-esteem

Parents will learn how stress effects parenting, how to offer self-esteem 'damage control', how to identify a 'toxic' parent, how to help your child cope with failure and the three keys to coaching your child towards a solid self-esteem.

Easy Tantrum Training

You will learn how to handle and prevent tantrums in toddlers (and even some adults!)

The Good Kid Game empowers parents with safety-net procedures for tantrums which produce least fuss and least upset. The Being Ready Routine is great for helping families beat the morning rush without panic, tears and tantrums!

ADULT HYPNOSIS AUDIOTAPES BY DR JANET HALL

Did you know that Dr Jan is a very experienced hypnotherapist? She believes very strongly in the power of the mind to assist in boosting your success and she has recorded many audiotapes which combine Jan's usual style of chatty, easily understood information, with a segment of hypnosis.

You Can Stop Smoking with Hypnosis

You know it's time! This audiotape will help you to boost your self-esteem and give you the willpower to quit smoking once and for all!

You Can Lose Weight with Hypnosis

You deserve to have a slim, fit and healthy body. Gain slimness easily and gain confidence in the power of your mind to achieve the results that you deserve.

Heart Healing: How To Heal a Broken Heart and Get on With a Successful Life

What do you do to cope when someone you loved has died or abandoned you?

Side 1 has an explanation of the healthiest way to let go of your upset.

Side 2 gives a unique hypnotic experience which allows your upset to be released and energises you to recommit to your right for maximum personal and relationship success.

You Can Have Total Confidence Through Relaxation

You can super-boost your self-esteem without even trying!

Side 1 gives you a classical relaxation meditation experience where you follow the healing light through your body so that you feel at peace with your world.

Side 2 is a power-boosting and inspiring coaching experience with Dr Jan.

ADULT MOTIVATION AND INFORMATION AUDIOTAPES BY DR JANET HALL

How To Stress-Proof Yourself and Succeed… Faster

With Stress-Proof Coaching you can learn to achieve your goals faster, with no burn-out.

Stop Sexual Harassment! It's Bad for Business!

Sexual Harassment can cost millions of dollars with job turn-over expenses, lost productivity and stress-related illness. This audio explains why sexual tension occurs in business and how to promote healthy sexual politics to create and environment that protects your business and investment.

FOR AVAILABILITY OF ALL DR JANET HALL PRODUCTS CONTACT:

Save Secretarial Service PO Box 5000

Middle Camberwell 3124

Phone: [03] 9888 6522 or Email: jrichard@bigpond.net.au